Correcting Paragraphs

Grammar Practice Workbook

Jenny Pearson

Correcting Paragraphs

Grammar Practice Workbook

Jenny Pearson

Copyright © 2019 Kivett Publishing

Kivett Publishing

ISBN: 978-1-941691-44-1

Juvenile > Language Arts > Grammar

TABLE OF CONTENTS

INTRODUCTION

Each exercise in this book consists of a short paragraph that contains five grammar or spelling mistakes. The first chapter illustrates a variety of common mistakes, while the third chapter includes worked-out examples. The first three chapters should serve as a helpful guide.

Reading paragraphs and searching for five common mistakes helps to develop fluency with grammar and spelling. That is why exercises like these are common in language arts classes at elementary and middle schools.

The exercises are double spaced so that there is room between the lines for students to identify their corrections. Space below each exercise allows students to rewrite the entire paragraph correctly. Check the answers with the key located at the back of the book.

COMMON MISTAKES

The spelling and grammar rules described in this book involve conventions followed in the United States.

Capitalization Examples

Mistake: begin a sentence with an uppercase letter.

Correct: Begin a sentence with an uppercase letter.

Mistake: She said, "this will be a great day."

Correct: She said, "This will be a great day."

Mistake: My dad calls me his "Little angel."

Correct: My dad calls me his "little angel."

Note that "little angel" is an incomplete thought.

Mistake: You bet i can do it.

Correct: You bet I can do it.

Mistake: Today we met mr. smith.

Correct: Today we met Mr. Smith.

Mistake: I asked Mom why your Dad is upset.

Correct: I asked Mom why your dad is upset.

Compare "my mom" to "Mom" and "your dad" to "Dad." It's uppercase only if used like a name.

Mistake: I'm from los angeles.

Correct: I'm from Los Angeles.

Mistake: The movie comes out on friday.

Correct: The movie comes out on Friday.

Mistake: My mom bought this on amazon.

Correct: My mom bought this on Amazon.

Mistake: Can you imagine climbing mount everest?

Correct: Can you imagine climbing Mount Everest?

Mistake: I enjoyed reading *the jungle book*.

Correct: I enjoyed reading *The Jungle Book*.

Mistake: Tomorrow is valentine's day.

Correct: Tomorrow is Valentine's Day.

Mistake: My grandfather fought in world war ii.

Correct: My grandfather fought in World War II.

Punctuation Examples

Mistake: Where did everybody go.

Correct: Where did everybody go?

Mistake: Did you know that Mr Rex is 7 ft tall?

Correct: Did you know that Mr. Rex is 7 ft. tall?

Mistake: Put the CD. in the DVD. player.

Correct: Put the CD in the DVD player.

Mistake: I cant believe it!

Correct: I can't believe it!

Mistake: She scratched between the cats' ears.

Correct: She scratched between the cat's ears.

Mistake: Our cat's tails have stripes.

Correct: Our cats' tails have stripes.

Since a cat only has one tail, this example must be referring to the tails of more than one cat.

Mistake: The cat licked it's paw.

Correct: The cat licked its paw.

Mistake: It was a cold windy afternoon.

Correct: It was a cold, windy afternoon.

Mistake: Dad can I please borrow the car?

Correct: Dad, can I please borrow the car?

Mistake: We brought plates cups and napkins.

Correct: We brought plates, cups, and napkins.

Correct: We brought plates, cups and napkins.

The comma after "cups" is considered optional.

Mistake: The wind was starting to blow hard but there was still work to be done.

Correct: The wind was starting to blow hard, but there was still work to be done.

Mistake: I was born in Kent Ohio on May 7 2011.

Correct: I was born in Kent, Ohio, on May 7, 2011.

Mistake: The blockbuster movie star Jack Gray signed his autograph for me.

Correct: The blockbuster movie star, Jack Gray, signed his autograph for me.

Mistake: Our new car unlike the previous model has cruise control.

Correct: Our new car, unlike the previous model, has cruise control.

Mistake: He said "It is cold outside today."

Correct: He said, "It is cold outside today."

Mistake: He said that "it is cold outside today."

Correct: He said that it is cold outside today.

Note how "said that" instead of just "said" makes a big difference.

Mistake: He said ",It's hot" ,and I replied ",It is".

Correct: He said, "It's hot," and I replied, "It is."

Mistake: Did you read an article entitled Big Ideas in the magazine Think Bigger?

Correct: Did you read an article entitled "Big Ideas" in the magazine *Think Bigger*?

Write the titles of shorter works in quotes, but italicize (or underline) the titles of longer works.

Mistake: This is my to do list.

Correct: This is my to-do list.

Mistake: I don't know what to-do.

Correct: I don't know what to do.

   Compare: Hyphenate "to-do list" because "to-do"

   serves as an adjective describing "list."

Mistake: That was very-good news.

Correct: That was very good news.

   Don't use a hyphen with very or with adverbs

   ending with "ly."

Mistake: Please bring; cheese, bread, and water.

Correct: Please bring: cheese, bread, and water.

Mistake: It was all she wanted; an opportunity.

Correct: It was all she wanted: an opportunity.

Mistake: Let me research it: then I'll get back to you.

Correct: Let me research it; then I'll get back to you.

   A semicolon joins two complete thoughts together

   if the thoughts are closely linked.

Grammar Examples

Mistake: When you hear thunder. Come back inside.

Correct: When you hear thunder, come back inside.

Mistake: We sang songs and danced and ate dinner.

Correct: We sang songs, danced, and ate dinner.

Correct: We sang songs, danced and ate dinner.

The comma after "danced" is considered optional.

Mistake: The leaves were beginning to turn red,

the days were starting to get shorter.

Correct: The leaves were beginning to turn red,

and the days were starting to get shorter.

Mistake: The paper and pencil is on the desk.

Correct: The paper and pencil are on the desk.

Mistake: Either my mom or dad are picking me up.

Correct: Either my mom or dad is picking me up.

Compare how the word "and" results in a plural

subject, but the word "or" does not.

Mistake: One box of roses cost twenty dollars.

Correct: One box of roses costs twenty dollars.

Cross out "of roses" and read the sentence. The subject is "one box," so the verb should be "costs."

Mistake: Some of the class are absent.

Correct: Some of the class is absent.

Mistake: Some of the students is absent.

Correct: Some of the students are absent.

Since the word "some" indicates a portion, it doesn't follow the previous crossing out rule.

Mistake: They didn't want no juice.

Correct: They didn't want juice.

Mistake: Here's the tickets that you will need.

Correct: Here are the tickets that you will need.

Mistake: More than one apple have spoiled.

Correct: More than one apple has spoiled.

Mistake: Everybody are present today.

Correct: Everybody is present today.

Mistake: Five days are a long time to wait.

Correct: Five days is a long time to wait.

Although "five days" seems like a plural, in this context it is considered as a single unit of time.

Mistake: He goes to the restaurant and ate lunch.

Correct: He went to the restaurant and ate lunch.

In this example, there was no logical reason for the tense to switch from present tense to past tense.

Mistake: Yesterday were Saturday.

Correct: Yesterday was Saturday.

Mistake: I wish today was Saturday.

Correct: I wish today were Saturday.

Mistake: If Sam was on time, we could begin.

Correct: If Sam were on time, we could begin.

A sentence that seems doubtful or wishful, or a nonfactual statement using "if" or "unless" uses the word "were" instead of "was" (or the word "be" instead of "are"). This is the subjunctive mood.

Mistake: The robbers were binded together.

Correct: The robbers were bound together.

Mistake: He choosed the second option.

Correct: He chose the second option.

Mistake: He has chosed the second option.

Correct: He has chosen the second option.

Mistake: He layed the book on the desk.

Correct: He laid the book on the desk.

Mistake: I lied down because I needed some rest.

Correct: I lay down because I needed some rest.

Mistake: I have lied down for a while.

Correct: I have lain down for a while.

Note that "lay" takes an object (like "book"), but "lie" doesn't. The past tense of "lay" is "laid." The past tense of "lie" is "lay" and the past participle of "lie" is "lain" (used with "has," "have," or "had").

Note that not telling the truth is a different use of the word "lie," for which the past tense is "lied."

Mistake: My father and me ate dinner together.

Correct: My father and I ate dinner together.

You wouldn't say, "Me ate dinner."

Mistake: They invited my father and I.

Correct: They invited my father and me.

You wouldn't say, "They invited I."

Mistake: She called I.

Correct: She called me.

Mistake: It was me.

Correct: It was I.

The verbs "am," "is," "are," "was," and "were" don't take an object. It will make sense if you try adding to the sentence. You would say, "It was I who did it," instead of, "It was me who did it."

Mistake: The man brought gifts, and his wife passed it out to everybody.

Correct: The man brought gifts, and his wife passed them out to everybody.

Mistake: We did it by ourself.

Correct: We did it by ourselves.

Mistake: I was talking to me.

Correct: I was talking to myself.

Mistake: The book belongs to Becky and myself.

Correct: The book belongs to Becky and me.

Mistake: My mother and myself enjoy dancing.

Correct: My mother and I enjoy dancing.

Mistake: She served toast to the guests with butter.

Correct: She served toast with butter to the guests.

Mistake: The child died of laughter nearly every

time his grandfather told that joke.

Correct: The child nearly died of laughter every

time his grandfather told that joke.

Mistake: Does the red or blue dress look best?

Correct: Does the red or blue dress look better?

When there are only two choices (like red or blue),
use the comparative instead of superlative form.

Mistake: She plays tennis good .

Correct: She plays tennis well.

Mistake: Your sister's drawing is well .

Correct: Your sister's drawing is good.

Mistake: The soldiers fought brave .

Correct: The soldiers fought bravely.

Mistake: He is remarkable intelligent.

Correct: He is remarkably intelligent.

An adjective modifies a noun or pronoun, while an adverb modifies a verb, adjective, or adverb. Many adverbs end with "ly," but a few (like "well") don't, and a few adjectives (like "friendly") end with "ly." A few words (like "fast" or "only") can act as either adjectives or adverbs.

Mistake: This dessert tastes deliciously .

Correct: This dessert tastes delicious.

Use adjectives with sensory verbs (like "taste," "look," or "feel").

Word Confusion Examples

Mistake: We went their on Thanksgiving Day.

Correct: We went there on Thanksgiving Day.

Mistake: There parents wouldn't allow it.

Correct: Their parents wouldn't allow it.

Mistake: That shirt costs to much.

Correct: That shirt costs too much.

Mistake: It sounded like a honest answer.

Correct: It sounded like an honest answer.

Mistake: My mother said that it would be alright.

Correct: My mother said that it would be all right.

Mistake: What tastes better then strawberry?

Correct: What tastes better than strawberry?

Mistake: One of the screws is lose.

Correct: One of the screws is loose.

Mistake: How did you loose the game?

Correct: How did you lose the game?

Mistake: Do we know whom wrote the note?

Correct: Do we know who wrote the note?

Mistake: Do we know who the book is about?

Correct: Do we know whom the book is about?

We would say, "He wrote the note," and, "The book is about him." Note that he/him is like who/whom.

Mistake: I past by the library on the way home.

Correct: I passed by the library on the way home.

Mistake: Pat earned less points than Tim.

Correct: Pat earned fewer points than Tim.

Mistake: Pat's score was fewer than Tim's.

Correct: Pat's score was less than Tim's.

The word "less" describes singular words, while the word "fewer" describes plural words.

Mistake: Take a deep breathe.

Correct: Take a deep breath.

Mistake: Try to breath naturally.

Correct: Try to breathe naturally.

Mistake: I need to lay down for a while.

Correct: I need to lie down for a while.

Mistake: Lie the book on the desk.

Correct: Lay the book on the desk.

The verb "lay" takes an object (like "book"), but the verb "lie" doesn't.

Mistake: The teacher doesn't except late papers.

Correct: The teacher doesn't accept late papers.

Mistake: Accept for me, the team is ready.

Correct: Except for me, the team is ready.

Mistake: The pennies were divided among Sarah and Virginia.

Correct: The pennies were divided between Sarah and Virginia.

Mistake: It was split between Raj, Taj, and Ram.

Correct: It was split among Raj, Taj, and Ram.

When dividing, use "between" for two people and use "among" for more than two people.

Spelling Examples

Mistake: The bilding was tall.

Correct: The building was tall.

Mistake: He was very nervus.

Correct: He was very nervous.

Mistake: The company is in too much det.

Correct: The company is in too much debt.

Mistake: Why are we wispering?

Correct: Why are we whispering?

Mistake: Please form two colums.

Correct: Please form two columns.

Mistake: I couldn't beleive it!

Correct: I couldn't believe it!

Mistake: She recieved a check for ten dollars.

Correct: She received a check for ten dollars.

Mistake: It was a large, grassy feild.

Correct: It was a large, grassy field.

Mistake: That really hurt my nuckles.

Correct: That really hurt my knuckles.

Mistake: I am shure.

Correct: I am sure.

Mistake: My aunt visited Egipt.

Correct: My aunt visited Egypt.

Mistake: He was born in Massachussetts.

Correct: He was born in Massachusetts.

Mistake: The dentist pulled two of my tooths.

Correct: The dentist pulled two of my teeth.

Mistake: She bought three loafs of bread.

Correct: She bought three loaves of bread.

Mistake: That price is a bargin.

Correct: That price is a bargain.

Mistake: Keep the whites seperate from the colors.

Correct: Keep the whites separate from the colors.

Mistake: That word was mispelled.

Correct: That word was misspelled.

STRATEGY

How do you find five mistakes in a paragraph?

Follow these steps:

- Read each paragraph carefully.

- Circle incorrect letters, punctuation marks, or words. Write in missing letters or punctuation.

- First correct mistakes that you are sure about.

- You are looking for exactly five mistakes.

- Ask yourself the following questions to help find the mistakes.

Question 1. Are there any capitalization mistakes?

- Check the first letter of each sentence.

- Also look for proper nouns.

Question 2. Are there any punctuation mistakes?

- Check every punctuation mark.

- Also look for missing punctuation marks.

Question 3. Are there any grammatical mistakes?

- Look for sentence fragments and run-on sentences.

- Check if the verb agrees with the subject. Examples where it doesn't agree include "he are" instead of "he is," "they was" instead of "they were," and "ice cubes melts" instead of "ice cubes melt."

- Are the pronouns (like "she," "it," or "himself") used correctly?

- Are adjectives and adverbs confused?

- Review the chapter with common mistakes.

Question 4. Are similar words confused?

- This is common with words that sound similar (like "no" and "know").

- It may help to look up the meaning of a word in a dictionary.

Question 5. Are there any spelling mistakes?

- It may help to check the spelling of a word using a dictionary.

EXAMPLES

Suggestions for using these examples:

- Cover up the corrected paragraph with a folded sheet of paper.

- Think your way through each paragraph as you read it.

- Try your best to identify the five mistakes.

- After you have made your best effort, read the corrected paragraph.

- Spend some time thinking about the corrections. Try to understand them.

- Below each corrected paragraph, you can find a summary of the mistakes with brief explanations.

- Were any of your answers incorrect? If so, try to learn from them. If not, use this to help boost your confidence.

EXAMPLE 1

I was pleasantly surprise when mrs Porter handed out are report cards today. Somehow I managed to earned an A in English.

I was pleasantly surprised when Mrs. Porter handed out our report cards today. Somehow I managed to earn an A in English.

1. surprised (past tense)
2. Mrs. (capitalize Mr., Mrs., Dr.)
3. Mrs. (this abbreviation ends with a period)
4. our (word confusion/the report cards belong to us)
5. earn (part of the infinitive "to earn")

EXAMPLE 2

We cant wait for this Weekend to begin. We will attend a concert friday night go to the beach Saturday, and played tennis Sunday.

We can't wait for this weekend to begin. We will attend a concert Friday night, go to the beach Saturday, and play tennis Sunday.

1. can't (contraction of "can not")

2. weekend (lowercase/not a proper noun)

3. Friday (capitalize a proper noun)

4. comma after "night" (separate the items of the list)

5. play ("We will play tennis Sunday")

EXAMPLE 3

The cat and dog was outside when it begin to rain. The cat hidden in a barrel but the dog ran around until it stopped raining

The cat and dog were outside when it began to rain. The cat hid in a barrel, but the dog ran around until it stopped raining.

1. were (two subjects, cat and dog)

2. began (the sentence began in the past tense)

3. hid (the past tense of "hide" is irregular)

4. comma (separate two clauses)

5. period (at the end of the sentence)

EXAMPLE 4

My freind and me went to the movie theater. We watched *sleepy cowboys*. My favorite parts of the movie was the popcorn.

My friend and I went to the movie theater. We watched Sleepy Cowboys. My favorite part of the movie was the popcorn.

1. friend (spelling)

2. I (part of the subject)

3. Sleepy (capitalize the movie title)

   (Note: When printing by hand, use underline instead of italics.)

4. Cowboys (capitalize the movie title)

5. part (singular/only one part is described)

EXAMPLE 5

She said that "the camping trip was packed with fun activities." She said I can't wait to go again next year.

She said that ⎸the camping trip was packed with fun activities.⎸She said⎸,⎸"⎸I can't wait to go again next year.⎸"

1. Don't use quotation marks after the word "that."
2. Also remove the end quotes.
3. Insert a comma before the quote begins.
4. Use quotation marks for this direct quote.
5. Also add end quotes.

PARAGRAPHS

Directions:

- Read each paragraph carefully.

- Search for five mistakes.

- Follow the strategy in Chapter 2.

- If you're stuck, browse through Chapters 1 and 3 to get some ideas.

- When you find a mistake, circle what is wrong and make a correction in the space above the line.

- Once you find five mistakes, rewrite the entire paragraph on the blank lines below.

- When you finish, check your answers in the back of the book.

- Were any of your answers incorrect? If so, try to learn from them. If not, use this to help boost your confidence.

PARAGRAPH 1

Today was me friends birthday. She invited myself over for her party. We played games ate cake, and danced too music.

_____

_____

_____

_____

_____

_____

_____

_____

PARAGRAPH 2

A butterfly with color full wings fluttered

threw the air it landed on a flower nearby.

a moment later it was flying again.

_____

_____

_____

_____

_____

_____

_____

_____

PARAGRAPH 3

Where did you by that bookmark. I cant take my eyes off of it. If I have a bookmark like that, I would be easy distracted.

_____

_____

_____

_____

_____

_____

_____

_____

PARAGRAPH 4

Lisa visited california in the Summer.

She went to the mountins the beach, and

disneyland.

_____

_____

_____

_____

_____

_____

_____

_____

PARAGRAPH 5

All of the student's noses were runny today.

The teacher asked the class are you allergic to

school?

_____

_____

_____

_____

_____

_____

_____

_____

_____

PARAGRAPH 6

I'll give it a try dad. Tomorrow I'll let you know whether or not you're idea works. wish my luck.

_____

_____

_____

_____

_____

_____

_____

_____

PARAGRAPH 7

The man was nervous when he recieved a phone call from dr. Carson but it turned out to be good news. The Doctor told him that his test results come back fine.

_____

_____

_____

_____

_____

_____

_____

_____

_____

PARAGRAPH 8

Dear Alice.

Please by milk and bread at the store on

you way home from school.

Love mom

_____

_____

_____

_____

_____

_____

_____

_____

PARAGRAPH 9

She threw the basketball. Into the basket.

Our team one the game. They made it to

the playoffs. Can you belief it!

_____

_____

_____

_____

_____

_____

_____

_____

PARAGRAPH 10

His toothbrush and comb is in the bag.

He all ready took a bath, he hasn't ate

dinner yet. Call myself when you get there.

_____

_____

_____

_____

_____

_____

_____

_____

_____

PARAGRAPH 11

The necklace and bracelet is in the drore.

Either the blue or green hat match those

shoes. All that remain is to look confidence.

_____

_____

_____

_____

_____

_____

_____

_____

PARAGRAPH 12

They were glad that the son was out because they had forgot there umbrellas. It was a splendid day too be out side.

_____

_____

_____

_____

_____

_____

_____

_____

PARAGRAPH 13

My sister and me get along good. We share our things we play game together, and she offers helpful advise when I need it.

_____

_____

_____

_____

_____

_____

_____

_____

PARAGRAPH 14

Most of the group were upset but I wasn't.

I didn't minded the bus was late: I needed

more time to study for the test.

_____

_____

_____

_____

_____

_____

_____

_____

PARAGRAPH 15

The man said "It looks like it will rain today". The woman responded "I hope not. I just washed my car". Just as she finished speaking, thunder sound in the distance.

_____

_____

_____

_____

_____

_____

_____

_____

PARAGRAPH 16

Just as it was begining to seem like a

never ending journey the travelers

emerged from the forrest. The familiar

vally below was a welcome sight.

_____
_____
_____
_____
_____
_____
_____
_____

PARAGRAPH 17

Mikes bicycle breaked on his way home.

When the breaks stopped working, he had

to walk. Fortunately, it was'nt to far.

_____

_____

_____

_____

_____

_____

_____

_____

PARAGRAPH 18

There's the boxes that we receive in the male last week. I careful layed the boxes on the table myself.

_____

_____

_____

_____

_____

_____

_____

_____

PARAGRAPH 19

The peanut had a very-hard shells. When

the man couldnt open it with his fingers,

he use a pair of plier.

_____

_____

_____

_____

_____

_____

_____

_____

PARAGRAPH 20

Harry did his chores Harry complete his homeworks assignment. Final he had time to relaxing.

_____

_____

_____

_____

_____

_____

_____

_____

PARAGRAPH 21

Paul ordered a ice cream sandwich Nancy

ordered two chocolate chip cookie, and

Doug ordered an vanilla shake.

_____

_____

_____

_____

_____

_____

_____

_____

PARAGRAPH 22

The carton of eggs go in the refrigerator,

the package of fruit go on the counter.

Thanks you for putting the grocery away.

_____

_____

_____

_____

_____

_____

_____

_____

PARAGRAPH 23

We don't have time for no games this

morning. We need too packs our suitcases.

Are father will be driving us to the airport

in half an hours.

_____

_____

_____

_____

_____

_____

_____

_____

PARAGRAPH 24

My grandmother knitted blanket for Rachel and I. Mine has bright orange flowers, while Rachel has brown teddy bares. Would you like to see them.

_____

_____

_____

_____

_____

_____

_____

_____

PARAGRAPH 25

There team is the best in the league: they only losed one game last year. tickets for the next game are all ready sold out.

_____

_____

_____

_____

_____

_____

_____

_____

_____

PARAGRAPH 26

Our teacher often says, "draw a digram to help see what is going on in the problem".

On todays math test it actual helped me.

_____

_____

_____

_____

_____

_____

_____

_____

PARAGRAPH 27

Your the third person Ive met whom

moved here from south Carolina. Would

your like a tour of our town?

_____

_____

_____

_____

_____

_____

_____

_____

_____

PARAGRAPH 28

My frend draws very good. Her pitchers

look incredible real. I wish that I had

artistically talent.

_____

_____

_____

_____

_____

_____

_____

_____

_____

PARAGRAPH 29

Member to where your jacket and mittens.

Its much colder out side this morning then

it has been all week.

PARAGRAPH 30

The kichen recently remodeled looks nice.

It is functional, to. Our family spend much

time in here now.

_____

_____

_____

_____

_____

_____

_____

_____

PARAGRAPH 31

I enjoyed reading Franz Kafka short

story, A Hunger Artist, but was unable

to make myself finish reading his famous

book The Trial.

_____

_____

_____

_____

_____

_____

_____

_____

PARAGRAPH 32

Everyone were too busy to come Saturday evening, but most of my friends is free Tomorrow morning. Thats why we change the date of the party.

PARAGRAPH 33

Closed your eyes. Take deep breathes. Feel your mussles relax. Say a first word that come to your mind.

_____

_____

_____

_____

_____

_____

_____

_____

_____

PARAGRAPH 34

She layed the notepad on the table, and then she lied down to take a nap, she was very more productive after some rest.

_____

_____

_____

_____

_____

_____

_____

_____

_____

PARAGRAPH 35

Please except my apology. I real did'nt

meaned to spill my drink on your shirt.

It were just an accident.

_____

_____

_____

_____

_____

_____

_____

_____

PARAGRAPH 36

According to the pythagorean theorem'

the sum of the squares of the leg of a right

triangle, equal the square of the hypotenuse.

_____

_____

_____

_____

_____

_____

_____

_____

PARAGRAPH 37

I goed to the zoo with my two brother. My

favorit part was watched the monkeys

chase a squirrel out of there cage.

_____

_____

_____

_____

_____

_____

_____

_____

_____

PARAGRAPH 38

A police car raced passed us with its siren blaring, when we past it a few minutes later, it was park behind a sports car.

PARAGRAPH 39

The teacher said that "she had to go to a meeting." However, she did say, please come back after the meeting. I will be happy to help you then.

_____

_____

_____

_____

_____

_____

_____

_____

_____

PARAGRAPH 40

The roller coaster slowly climb high up in the sky. Once it reached the top, it speed down and went through a loop. It was funny when my dad said I want my mommy.

_____

_____

_____

_____

_____

_____

_____

_____

PARAGRAPH 41

My family and me watched a whale shows.

When the wale swam by, water splashes

onto my sister and I.

_____

_____

_____

_____

_____

_____

_____

_____

_____

PARAGRAPH 42

Tomorrow is independence day. Our Dad

will barbecue hot dogs and hamburgers

at night we will watch fireworks.

_____

_____

_____

_____

_____

_____

_____

_____

PARAGRAPH 43

We bilt this treehouse by ourself. If you want to come in, youll need to say the secret passcode. Gess what it is?

PARAGRAPH 44

Please be care full not to brake the meer

because seven years are a long time to

had bad luck.

_____

_____

_____

_____

_____

_____

_____

_____

_____

PARAGRAPH 45

Its to late to work on the project now.

Tomorrow morning after a good nights

sleep we will finish it.

_____

_____

_____

_____

_____

_____

_____

_____

PARAGRAPH 46

That is a very-bad idea. The long term benefits dont justify the cost. Whom else has a sugestion?

_____

_____

_____

_____

_____

_____

_____

_____

_____

PARAGRAPH 47

We used our spare change to by a bag of candy. The chocolates were split between Jeff Tom, and Elle. The rest were divided among Larry and Valerie.

_____

_____

_____

_____

_____

_____

_____

_____

PARAGRAPH 48

Mark would you take down the tents? Liz

would you pack our belonging in the bags?

I'll fix the flat tire. Hopeful, we can get

out of here before the storm came.

_____

_____

_____

_____

_____

_____

_____

_____

_____

PARAGRAPH 49

Here's the five dollar that I owe you. Thank

for lending me the mony. I don't know

how I would have got home otherwise.

_____

_____

_____

_____

_____

_____

_____

_____

PARAGRAPH 50

In sciense class, Ms Kay drop a penny and

a feather in a vaccum tube. To my suprise,

they hit the bottom at the same time.

_____

_____

_____

_____

_____

_____

_____

_____

PARAGRAPH 51

A frog sitting on a lily pad sudden sticked

it's long tung out of its mouth and caught

a unsuspecting fly.

_____

_____

_____

_____

_____

_____

_____

_____

PARAGRAPH 52

My brother is moving to Trenton New Jersey on August 12 2019. After that, i got to move into his room.

_____

_____

_____

_____

_____

_____

_____

_____

PARAGRAPH 53

"Happy Birthday dad," I said. My father closed his eyes, silent made a wish, and blowed out all of the candles.

PARAGRAPH 54

Please inform the boys' that their late for

dinner. Thats the third time this weak. If

it happened again, they will be grounded.

_____

_____

_____

_____

_____

_____

_____

_____

PARAGRAPH 55

Everybody were excited win the wide reciever caught the touchdown pass to win the football game. That was the noisier that the stadium has ever bin.

_____

_____

_____

_____

_____

_____

_____

_____

PARAGRAPH 56

I didn't miss one class accept for the weak

when I had the flew, but that turned out to

be the more important class of the semester.

That material will be on half of the final

_____

_____

_____

_____

_____

_____

_____

_____

_____

PARAGRAPH 57

Be very quite. Sneak across the hallway.

Tiptoe down the stares. Grab the teddy

bare. Retrace your steps. To your room.

_____

_____

_____

_____

_____

_____

_____

_____

PARAGRAPH 58

I love your blanket because it feels softly.

Wear did you get it. I'm saving my money

so that I can by one, to.

_____

_____

_____

_____

_____

_____

_____

PARAGRAPH 59

Cash or credit work. The vending machine excepts doller bills as well as credit cards. But it charges a credit card fee of 50 cents.

_____

_____

_____

_____

_____

_____

_____

_____

PARAGRAPH 60

My mother calls this room her, "Lady cave."

Im not quiet sure what that means, but I do

no that only females go in that room.

_____

_____

_____

_____

_____

_____

_____

_____

PARAGRAPH 61

Felix what are you doing. You just put a

carton of milk in the cupboard? Please

pay attention, too what you are doing.

_____

_____

_____

_____

_____

_____

_____

_____

_____

PARAGRAPH 62

I'm very excite today! Their aren't much

pages left to reed in my book. I will finally

learn how the story end.

PARAGRAPH 63

According to the Article, we need; a large cardboard box packing tape, a wire hanger, and sissors. We can use these material to make a cat toy.

_____

_____

_____

_____

_____

_____

_____

_____

PARAGRAPH 64

"The rake and broom is in the shed. Please

bring it here, dear," said the wife. "No

problem honey," the husband replied. "I'll

be there in a few minutes."

_____

_____

_____

_____

_____

_____

_____

_____

PARAGRAPH 65

One can of tomatos are for my grandma, but your welcome to take the rest what are you planning to bake with them?

_____

_____

_____

_____

_____

_____

_____

_____

PARAGRAPH 66

If it wasn't raining, we could play outside.

Sense it is raining, lets play inside. Would

you like to play a bored games?

_____

_____

_____

_____

_____

_____

_____

_____

PARAGRAPH 67

My math grade has rised from 72% to 86% in just three week. Im glad were no longer working with fraction.

_____

_____

_____

_____

_____

_____

_____

PARAGRAPH 68

I already ate mom. Kelly and me made

peenut butter sandwiches when we come

home from school.

_____

_____

_____

_____

_____

_____

_____

_____

_____

PARAGRAPH 69

Between the solid tie and the stripped tie,

witch do you like best. I'm nervess about

my interview today.

_____

_____

_____

_____

_____

_____

_____

_____

PARAGRAPH 70

It was the worse round of golf I have never played. I couldn't make the ball go strait. I need to practise most often.

_____

_____

_____

_____

_____

_____

_____

_____

_____

PARAGRAPH 71

Warming up in a cosy blanket next to the fireplace feeled wonderful after coming in from the blizard on a day like this, reading a book was more fun than being outside.

_____

_____

_____

_____

_____

_____

_____

_____

_____

PARAGRAPH 72

Does you remember what it was like when your learned how to ride a bicicle? Do you fall several time before you figured out how to ride it?

_____

_____

_____

_____

_____

_____

_____

_____

PARAGRAPH 73

Coach O'Riley penned a bronze metal on Shawn' shirt cause Shawn finishes the race in third place.

_____

_____

_____

_____

_____

_____

_____

_____

PARAGRAPH 74

According to sientists, the rinoceros is an distant cosin of the horse. Those seem like strange reletives. Do you believe it?

_____

_____

_____

_____

_____

_____

_____

_____

_____

PARAGRAPH 75

Sally holded a seashell up to her ear. She heared a sound inside of the seashell reminds her of the oshen.

_____

_____

_____

_____

_____

_____

_____

_____

PARAGRAPH 76

Which letter doesnt appear in any of the names of the fifty states of the United states of America? the anser is Q

_____

_____

_____

_____

_____

_____

_____

_____

PARAGRAPH 77

Seperate the white laundry from the colors.

Set a garbage outside Washed the dishes.

When you finish your chores you may play.

_____

_____

_____

_____

_____

_____

_____

_____

PARAGRAPH 78

Do you beleive that there are life on other planet in the universe or do you think that life only exist in our solar system?

_____

_____

_____

_____

_____

_____

_____

_____

_____

Paragraphs

PARAGRAPH 79

Our class took a feild trip to the muzeum of history. I was suprised that they had the cherry tree that george Washington had chop down. (I'm joking, of course.)

_____

_____

_____

_____

_____

_____

_____

_____

110

PARAGRAPH 80

"Tiffany, please help me find my phone"

said her mother. "Okay mom" Tiffany

replied. Tiffany found her mothers

phone on the bathroom counter.

_____

_____

_____

_____

_____

_____

_____

_____

PARAGRAPH 81

the man ordered coffee from the waitress

with cream. He red the newspaper wile he

waited

_____

_____

_____

_____

_____

_____

_____

_____

_____

PARAGRAPH 82

Nuts grows on trees but peanuts grows underground. Thats why peanuts aren't nuts. Doesn't that seems nutty?

_____

_____

_____

_____

_____

_____

_____

_____

PARAGRAPH 83

Robert held the kite up hi while Gloria run with the string. a moment later, the kite was flyin hi.

PARAGRAPH 84

Babysitting had seem like a good idea until her smelled a awful odor. It was timed to change her first diper.

_____

_____

_____

_____

_____

_____

_____

_____

_____

PARAGRAPH 85

"I though this was a freeway" said the

driver "but today it seems most like a

parking lot.

_____

_____

_____

_____

_____

_____

_____

_____

PARAGRAPH 86

Why was all of the children giggling? Were

someone telling jokes? Were there a clown?

No, they was just watching a cartoons.

_____

_____

_____

_____

_____

_____

_____

_____

PARAGRAPH 87

Yesterday my father brought home a pet parrot. I wanted to name him butter but it would have sounded funny if he learned to say Butter wants a cracker.

_____

_____

_____

_____

_____

_____

_____

_____

PARAGRAPH 88

Brillyant minds made the technology that we enjoy today possibly. Its amazing that humans can fly, heal wounds, make robots, communicate instant across the globe.

_____

_____

_____

_____

_____

_____

_____

_____

PARAGRAPH 89

Accept for the elephant's trunks which were rather bizzy the elephants barely moved.

_____

_____

_____

_____

_____

_____

_____

_____

_____

PARAGRAPH 90

Buzzing bumblebees past by our head.

Not wanting to bee stinged, we quickly

went inside and close the door.

_____

_____

_____

_____

_____

_____

_____

_____

PARAGRAPH 91

If the team doesn't score soon, they would loose the game. There defense have been great, but there offense needs improvement.

PARAGRAPH 92

Donald had less chores to do than Ronald.

It didn't seem fare. Ronald planed to ask

him father bout it when he finished.

_____

_____

_____

_____

_____

_____

_____

_____

PARAGRAPH 93

Their was one thing he wanted more then nothing else in the world; the aproval of his parents.

_____

_____

_____

_____

_____

_____

_____

_____

_____

PARAGRAPH 94

Our picture has a devastating curve-ball, but for it to be affective, he needs to work on the commend of his four seam fastball.

_____

_____

_____

_____

_____

_____

_____

PARAGRAPH 95

Water an carbon dioxide reacts together in plant to forming glucose and diatomic oxygen gas in photosynthesis. This process is essential for life as we knew it.

_____

_____

_____

_____

_____

_____

_____

_____

PARAGRAPH 96

My grandfather says that he need to lay down to take a nap. After he rest for a while, he will took us to the park. It will be about a hour from now.

_____

_____

_____

_____

_____

_____

_____

_____

PARAGRAPH 97

He come outside to get a breathe of fresh air. The patio was fool: evidently other peoples had the same idea.

_____

_____

_____

_____

_____

_____

_____

_____

PARAGRAPH 98

the cat has lied down on that pillow all day.

Its time for the cat too wake up and get some

exercize.

_____

_____

_____

_____

_____

_____

_____

_____

PARAGRAPH 99

Mel made valentines' day cards and past

it out to her friends. Mel's friends also gave

cards to her.

PARAGRAPH 100

To who did you adress the envelope? Is it somebody I known? What did you put in side of the envelope

_____

_____

_____

_____

_____

_____

_____

_____

PARAGRAPH 101

If Elizabeth was here, she would know exact what to do. Well just have to try our best. Does anybody have a sujestion.

_____

_____

_____

_____

_____

_____

_____

_____

_____

ANSWER KEY

Note: Sometimes there is more than one way to correct a mistake. For example, "She didn't lose none," could be, "She didn't lose any," or, "She lost none."

Paragraph 1 (page 32)

Today was my friend's birthday. She invited me over for her party. We played games, ate cake, and danced to music.

Paragraph 2 (page 33)

A butterfly with colorful wings fluttered through the air. It landed on a flower nearby. A moment later it was flying again.

Paragraph 3 (page 34)

Where did you buy that bookmark? I can't take my eyes off of it. If I had a bookmark like that, I would be easily distracted.

Paragraph 4 (page 35)

Lisa visited California in the summer.

She went to the mountains, the beach, and

Disneyland.

Paragraph 5 (page 36)

All of the students' noses were runny today.

The teacher asked the class, "Are you allergic to

school?"

Paragraph 6 (page 37)

I'll give it a try, Dad. Tomorrow I'll let you

know whether or not your idea works.

Wish me luck.

Paragraph 7 (page 38)

The man was nervous when he received a

phone call from Dr. Carson, but it turned

out to be good news. The doctor told him

that his test results came back fine.

Paragraph 8 (page 39)

Dear Alice,

Please buy milk and bread at the store on

your way home from school.

Love, Mom

Paragraph 9 (page 40)

She threw the basketball into the basket.

Our team won the game. They made it to

the playoffs. Can you believe it?

Paragraph 10 (page 41)

His toothbrush and comb are in the bag.

He already took a bath, but he hasn't eaten

dinner yet. Call me when you get there.

Paragraph 11 (page 42)

The necklace and bracelet are in the drawer.

Either the blue or green hat matches those

shoes. All that remains is to look confident.

Paragraph 12 (page 43)

They were glad that the sun was out because they had forgotten their umbrellas. It was a splendid day to be outside.

Paragraph 13 (page 44)

My sister and I get along well. We share our things, we play games together, and she offers helpful advice when I need it.

Paragraph 14 (page 45)

Most of the group was upset, but I wasn't. I didn't mind that the bus was late; I needed more time to study for the test.

Paragraph 15 (page 46)

The man said, "It looks like it will rain today." The woman responded, "I hope not. I just washed my car." Just as she finished speaking, thunder sounded in the distance.

Paragraph 16 (page 47)

Just as it was beginning to seem like a never-ending journey, the travelers emerged from the forest. The familiar valley below was a welcome sight.

Paragraph 17 (page 48)

Mike's bicycle broke on his way home. When the brakes stopped working, he had to walk. Fortunately, it wasn't too far.

Paragraph 18 (page 49)

There are the boxes that we received in the mail last week. I carefully laid the boxes on the table myself.

Paragraph 19 (page 50)

The peanut had a very hard shell. When the man couldn't open it with his fingers, he used a pair of pliers.

Paragraph 20 (page 51)

Harry did his chores. Harry completed his homework assignment. Finally he had time to relax.

Paragraph 21 (page 52)

Paul ordered an ice-cream sandwich, Nancy ordered two chocolate chip cookies, and Doug ordered a vanilla shake.

Paragraph 22 (page 53)

The carton of eggs goes in the refrigerator, and the package of fruit goes on the counter. Thank you for putting the groceries away.

Paragraph 23 (page 54)

We don't have time for games this morning. We need to pack our suitcases. Our father will be driving us to the airport in half an hour.

Paragraph 24 (page 55)

My grandmother knitted blankets for Rachel and me. Mine has bright orange flowers, while Rachel's has brown teddy bears. Would you like to see them?

Paragraph 25 (page 56)

Their team is the best in the league; they only lost one game last year. Tickets for the next game are already sold out.

Paragraph 26 (page 57)

Our teacher often says, "Draw a diagram to help see what is going on in the problem." On today's math test it actually helped me.

Paragraph 27 (page 58)

You're the third person I've met who moved here from South Carolina. Would you like a tour of our town?

Paragraph 28 (page 59)

My friend draws very well. Her pictures look incredibly real. I wish that I had artistic talent.

Paragraph 29 (page 60)

Remember to wear your jacket and mittens. It's much colder outside this morning than it has been all week.

Paragraph 30 (page 61)

The kitchen, recently remodeled, looks nice. It is functional, too. Our family spends much time in here now.

Paragraph 31 (page 62)

I enjoyed reading Franz Kafka's short story, "A Hunger Artist," but was unable to make myself finish reading his famous book, *The Trial*. (Note: When printing by hand, use underline instead of italics.)

Paragraph 32 (page 63)

Everyone was too busy to come Saturday evening, but most of my friends are free tomorrow morning. That's why we changed the date of the party.

Paragraph 33 (page 64)

Close your eyes. Take deep breaths. Feel your muscles relax. Say the first word that comes to your mind.

Paragraph 34 (page 65)

She laid the notepad on the table, and then she lay down to take a nap. She was much more productive after some rest. (Note: "Lay" vs. "lie" is discussed in Chapter 1.)

Paragraph 35 (page 66)

Please accept my apology. I really didn't mean to spill my drink on your shirt. It was just an accident.

Paragraph 36 (page 67)

According to the Pythagorean theorem,
the sum of the squares of the legs of a right
triangle equals the square of the hypotenuse.
(Note: Some guides would capitalize Theorem.)

Paragraph 37 (page 68)

I went to the zoo with my two brothers. My
favorite part was watching the monkeys
chase a squirrel out of their cage.

Paragraph 38 (page 69)

A police car raced past us with its siren
blaring. When we passed it a few minutes
later, it was parked behind a sports car.

Paragraph 39 (page 70)

The teacher said that she had to go to a
meeting. However, she did say, "Please
come back after the meeting. I will be
happy to help you then."

Paragraph 40 (page 71)

The roller coaster slowly climbed high up in the sky. Once it reached the top, it sped down and went through a loop. It was funny when my dad said, "I want my mommy."

Paragraph 41 (page 72)

My family and I watched a whale show. When the whale swam by, water splashed onto my sister and me.

Paragraph 42 (page 73)

Tomorrow is Independence Day. Our dad will barbecue hot dogs and hamburgers. At night we will watch fireworks.

Paragraph 43 (page 74)

We built this treehouse by ourselves. If you want to come in, you'll need to say the secret passcode. Guess what it is.

Paragraph 44 (page 75)

Please be careful not to break the mirror because seven years is a long time to have bad luck.

Paragraph 45 (page 76)

It's too late to work on the project now. Tomorrow morning, after a good night's sleep, we will finish it.

Paragraph 46 (page 77)

That is a very bad idea. The long-term benefits don't justify the cost. Who else has a suggestion?

Paragraph 47 (page 78)

We used our spare change to buy a bag of candy. The chocolates were split among Jeff, Tom, and Elle. The rest was divided between Larry and Valerie.

Paragraph 48 (page 79)

Mark, would you take down the tents? Liz,

would you pack our belongings in the bags?

I'll fix the flat tire. Hopefully, we can get

out of here before the storm comes.

Paragraph 49 (page 80)

Here are the five dollars that I owe you. Thanks

for lending me the money. I don't know

how I would have gotten home otherwise.

Paragraph 50 (page 81)

In science class, Ms. Kay dropped a penny and

a feather in a vacuum tube. To my surprise,

they hit the bottom at the same time.

Paragraph 51 (page 82)

A frog sitting on a lily pad suddenly stuck

its long tongue out of its mouth and caught

an unsuspecting fly.

Paragraph 52 (page 83)

My brother is moving to Trenton, New

Jersey, on August 12, 2019. After that, I

get to move into his room.

Paragraph 53 (page 84)

"Happy birthday, Dad," I said. My father

closed his eyes, silently made a wish, and

blew out all of the candles.

Paragraph 54 (page 85)

Please inform the boys that they're late for

dinner. That's the third time this week. If

it happens again, they will be grounded.

Paragraph 55 (page 86)

Everybody was excited when the wide

receiver caught the touchdown pass to

win the football game. That was the

noisiest that the stadium has ever been.

Paragraph 56 (page 87)

I didn't miss one class except for the week when I had the flu, but that turned out to be the most important class of the semester. That material will be on half of the final.

Paragraph 57 (page 88)

Be very quiet. Sneak across the hallway. Tiptoe down the stairs. Grab the teddy bear. Retrace your steps to your room.

Paragraph 58 (page 89)

I love your blanket because it feels soft. Where did you get it? I'm saving my money so that I can buy one, too.

Paragraph 59 (page 90)

Cash or credit works. The vending machine accepts dollar bills as well as credit cards, but it charges a credit card fee of 50 cents.

Paragraph 60 (page 91)

My mother calls this room her "lady cave."
I'm not quite sure what that means, but I do
know that only females go in that room.

Paragraph 61 (page 92)

Felix, what are you doing? You just put a
carton of milk in the cupboard. Please
pay attention to what you are doing.

Paragraph 62 (page 93)

I'm very excited today! There aren't many
pages left to read in my book. I will finally
learn how the story ends.

Paragraph 63 (page 94)

According to the article, we need: a large
cardboard box, packing tape, a wire hanger,
and scissors. We can use these materials to
make a cat toy.

Paragraph 64 (page 95)

"The rake and broom are in the shed. Please bring them here, Dear," said the wife. "No problem, Honey," the husband replied. "I'll be there in a few minutes."

Paragraph 65 (page 96)

One can of tomatoes is for my grandma, but you're welcome to take the rest. What are you planning to bake with them?

Paragraph 66 (page 97)

If it weren't raining, we could play outside. Since it is raining, let's play inside. Would you like to play a board game? (Note: See the subjunctive mood discussed in Chapter 1.)

Paragraph 67 (page 98)

My math grade has risen from 72% to 86% in just three weeks. I'm glad we're no longer working with fractions.

Paragraph 68 (page 99)

I already ate, Mom. Kelly and I made peanut butter sandwiches when we came home from school.

Paragraph 69 (page 100)

Between the solid tie and the striped tie, which do you like better? I'm nervous about my interview today.

Paragraph 70 (page 101)

It was the worst round of golf I have ever played. I couldn't make the ball go straight. I need to practice more often.

Paragraph 71 (page 102)

Warming up in a cozy blanket next to the fireplace felt wonderful after coming in from the blizzard. On a day like this, reading a book was more fun than being outside.

Paragraph 72 (page 103)

Do you remember what it was like when you learned how to ride a bicycle? Did you fall several times before you figured out how to ride it?

Paragraph 73 (page 104)

Coach O'Riley pinned a bronze medal on Shawn's shirt because Shawn finished the race in third place.

Paragraph 74 (page 105)

According to scientists, the rhinoceros is a distant cousin of the horse. Those seem like strange relatives. Do you believe it?

Paragraph 75 (page 106)

Sally held a seashell up to her ear. She heard a sound inside of the seashell that reminded her of the ocean.

Paragraph 76 (page 107)

Which letter doesn't appear in any of the names of the fifty states of the United States of America? The answer is Q.

Paragraph 77 (page 108)

Separate the white laundry from the colors. Set the garbage outside. Wash the dishes. When you finish your chores, you may play.

Paragraph 78 (page 109)

Do you believe that there is life on other planets in the universe, or do you think that life only exists in our solar system?

Paragraph 79 (page 110)

Our class took a field trip to the museum of history. I was surprised that they had the cherry tree that George Washington had chopped down. (I'm joking, of course.)

Paragraph 80 (page 111)

"Tiffany, please help me find my phone," said her mother. "Okay, Mom," Tiffany replied. Tiffany found her mother's phone on the bathroom counter.

Paragraph 81 (page 112)

The man ordered coffee with cream from the waitress. He read the newspaper while he waited.

Paragraph 82 (page 113)

Nuts grow on trees, but peanuts grow underground. That's why peanuts aren't nuts. Doesn't that seem nutty?

Paragraph 83 (page 114)

Robert held the kite up high while Gloria ran with the string. A moment later, the kite was flying high.

Paragraph 84 (page 115)

Babysitting had seem|ed| like a good idea until |she| smelled |an| awful odor. It was |time| to change her first |diaper|.

Paragraph 85 (page 116)

"I |thought| this was a freeway|,|" said the driver|,| "but today it seems |more| like a parking lot.|"|

Paragraph 86 (page 117)

Why |were| all of the children giggling? |Was| someone telling jokes? |Was| there a clown? No, they |were| just watching a |cartoon|.

Paragraph 87 (page 118)

Yesterday my father brought home a pet parrot. I wanted to name him |Butter|, but it would have sounded funny if he learned to say|,| |"|Butter wants a cracker."

Paragraph 88 (page 119)

Brilliant minds made the technology that we enjoy today possible. It's amazing that humans can fly, heal wounds, make robots, and communicate instantly across the globe.

Paragraph 89 (page 120)

Except for the elephants' trunks, which were rather busy, the elephants barely moved.

Paragraph 90 (page 121)

Buzzing bumblebees passed by our heads. Not wanting to be stung, we quickly went inside and closed the door.

Paragraph 91 (page 122)

If the team doesn't score soon, they will lose the game. Their defense has been great, but their offense needs improvement.

Paragraph 92 (page 123)

Donald had fewer chores to do than Ronald.
It didn't seem fair. Ronald planned to ask
his father about it when he finished.

Paragraph 93 (page 124)

There was one thing he wanted more than
anything else in the world: the approval of
his parents.

Paragraph 94 (page 125)

Our pitcher has a devastating curve ball, but
for it to be effective, he needs to work on the
command of his four-seam fastball.

Paragraph 95 (page 126)

Water and carbon dioxide react together
in plants to form glucose and diatomic
oxygen gas in photosynthesis. This process
is essential for life as we know it.

Paragraph 96 (page 127)

My grandfather says that he needs to lie down to take a nap. After he rests for a while, he will take us to the park. It will be about an hour from now. (Note: "Lay" vs. "lie" is discussed in Chapter 1.)

Paragraph 97 (page 128)

He came outside to get a breath of fresh air. The patio was full; evidently other people had the same idea.

Paragraph 98 (page 129)

The cat has lain down on that pillow all day. It's time for the cat to wake up and get some exercise.

Paragraph 99 (page 130)

Mel made Valentine's Day cards and passed them out to her friends. Mel's friends also gave cards to her.

Paragraph 100 (page 131)

To whom did you address the envelope? Is it somebody I know? What did you put inside of the envelope? (Note: "Who" vs. "whom" is discussed in Chapter 1.)

Paragraph 101 (page 132)

If Elizabeth were here, she would know exactly what to do. We'll just have to try our best. Does anybody have a suggestion? (Note: See the subjunctive mood discussed in Chapter 1.)

INDEX

A

B

C

D

E

K

P

Q

R

S

T

U

CURSIVE HANDWRITING

It's never too late to learn cursive handwriting.

- Learn how to write the cursive alphabet.

- Practice writing words, phrases, and sentences.

- Challenge yourself to remember how to write each letter in cursive.

- Writing prompts offer additional practice.

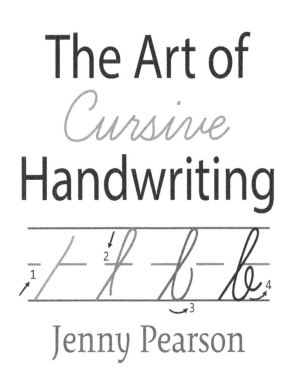

EXPRESS YOURSELF

Practice your writing skills with this composition writing prompts workbook. This book includes:

- a healthy variety of writing prompts.

- literary devices like similes and metaphors.

- a good mix of short answers with composition practice so as not to seem too intimidating.

- different forms of writing, such as opinions, descriptions, interviews, and short stories.

EXPRESS YOURSELF
Composition Writing Prompts Workbook

ideas · emotions · memories · issues
feelings · opinions · goals · thoughts
hopes · dreams · senses · vision

Jenny Pearson

SPELLING AND PHONICS

Spelling and phonics go hand-in-hand together:

- In *The Art of Spelling*, you learn techniques for how to spell a word after you've heard it spoken.

- In *The Art of Phonics*, you learn techniques for how to pronounce a word that you see in writing.

<table>
<tr><td colspan="2">The Art of
PHONICS</td></tr>
<tr><td>tough</td><td>through</td></tr>
<tr><td>though</td><td>thorough</td></tr>
<tr><td>thought</td><td>throughout</td></tr>
<tr><td colspan="2">Jenny Pearson</td></tr>
</table>

<table>
<tr><td colspan="3">The Art of
SPELLING</td></tr>
<tr><td>s</td><td>spag</td><td>spaghet</td></tr>
<tr><td>sp</td><td>spagh</td><td>spaghett</td></tr>
<tr><td>spa</td><td>spaghe</td><td>spaghetti</td></tr>
<tr><td colspan="3">Jenny Pearson</td></tr>
</table>

COLORING BOOKS

Coloring books aren't just for kids. They are popular among teens and adults, too. Coloring provides a relaxing way to take your mind off of stress, and lets you use your creativity.

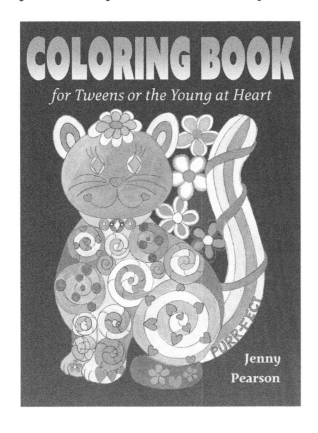

Made in the USA
Las Vegas, NV
08 September 2023

77237193R00096